The Oklahoma City Bombing: The History of the Deadliest Domestic Terrorist Attack in American History

By Charles River Editors

A picture of the Alfred P. Murrah Building after the attack

About Charles River Editors

Charles River Editors provides superior editing and original writing services across the digital publishing industry, with the expertise to create digital content for publishers across a vast range of subject matter. In addition to providing original digital content for third party publishers, we also republish civilization's greatest literary works, bringing them to new generations of readers via ebooks.

Introduction

The building before the attack

The Oklahoma City Bombing (April 19, 1995)

*Includes pictures

*Includes primary accounts of the attack

*Includes online resources and a bibliography for further reading

*Includes a table of contents

"Think about the people as if they were storm troopers in Star Wars. They may be individually innocent, but they are guilty because they work for the Evil Empire." – Timothy McVeigh

Two days after Ramzi Yousef's attack on the World Trade Center in 1993, federal agents from the Bureau of Alcohol, Tobacco and Firearms (ATF), the FBI and the Texas National Guard surrounded the Mount Carmel Center compound outside of Waco, Texas. They were there to search the property of the Branch Davidians, a religious cult, due to allegations that cult members were sexually abusing children and had assault weapons. When they began searching, the Branch Davidians, led by David Koresh, fired on them, starting a firefight and a nearly two month long siege of the compound.

The siege of the compound ended on April 19, 1993 with the deaths of over 75 cult members, including children, and in the wake of the event there was a lot of soul searching, but in addition to influencing how the government approached potential future conflicts with other groups, Waco's most important legacy was that it enraged people who already had an anti-government bent. As it turned out, the most notable was a young Gulf War veteran named Timothy McVeigh, who came to Waco during the siege and shouted his support for gun rights.

After the siege ended, McVeigh was determined to strike back at the federal government. In 1994, McVeigh and an old Army buddy, Michael Fortier, decided they would bomb the Alfred P. Murrah Federal Building in Oklahoma City because several federal agencies had offices inside, including the ATF. With the help of Terry Nichols, McVeigh constructed a bomb out of fertilizer that weighed over two tons and placed it in a rented Ryder truck, the same company Ramzi Yousef had rented a van from.

At 9:00 a.m. on April 19, 1995, the second anniversary of the end of the siege in Waco, McVeigh's bomb exploded with a force so powerful that it registered seismic readings across much of Oklahoma and could be heard 50 miles away. The explosion killed 168 people, including young children in the building's day-care center. McVeigh was captured shortly after the explosion, and he never displayed remorse for his actions. When he later learned about the day-care center, McVeigh called the children "collateral damage."

At the time, the bombing was the deadliest terrorist attack on American soil in history, and McVeigh was executed on June 11, 2001, three months before the bombing became the second deadliest terrorist attack on American soil in history.

The Oklahoma City Bombing: The History of the Deadliest Domestic Terrorist Attack in American History chronicles the notorious terrorist attack. Along with pictures of important people, places, and events, you will learn about the Oklahoma City bombing like never before.

The Oklahoma City Bombing: The History of the Deadliest Domestic Terrorist Attack in American History

About Charles River Editors

Introduction

Chapter 1: Distaste for the Federal Government

"On April 19th, 1993, that's four years ago…there was another great tragedy in American history. It occurred at Waco, Texas. That's the day that many lives were lost when the Branch Davidian compound burned down. But it was more than just a tragedy to McVeigh. You'll hear testimony from McVeigh's friends that he visited Waco during the siege and that he went back after the fire and that he had already harbored a great dislike and distaste for the federal government. They imposed taxes and the Brady Bill, and there were various other reasons that he had disliked the federal government. But the tragedy at Waco really sparked his anger; and as time passed, he became more and more and more outraged at the government, which he held responsible for the deaths at Waco. And he told people that the federal government had intentionally murdered people at Waco, they murdered the Davidians at Waco. He described the incident as the government's declaration of war against the American people. He wrote letters declaring that the government had drawn, quote, 'first blood,' unquote, at Waco; and he predicted there would be a violent revolution against the American government. As he put it, blood would flow in the streets." – Joseph Hartzler, prosecutor in the case against McVeigh

In February 1993, President Bill Clinton had only been in office for a few weeks when one of the most important events of his presidency began to take shape. Ironically, it would involve a group that the vast majority of Americans had never heard of and knew absolutely nothing about.

The Branch Davidians were an obscure religious sect located in Texas, but members of the group led by David Koresh in Waco, Texas stockpiled enough weaponry to catch the attention of the federal government. The U.S. Bureau of Alcohol, Tobacco, Firearms and Explosives (ATF) ultimately decided to serve arrest and search warrants at the compound for the possession of illegal weapons, even though they fully expected it would require a raid that could potentially turn fatal.

The ATF hoped to use the element of surprise when it commenced the raid on February 28, but the Branch Davidians were ready for them, which led to an intense firefight between the two sides that resulted in the deaths of 4 ATF agents and a number of Branch Davidians. With that, the FBI got involved, and federal agents settled in for a standoff that would last about 50 days, trying everything from negotiating to using sleep deprivation tactics to coerce the Branch Davidians into ending the confrontation. Finally, on April 19, government agents breached the compound's walls and tried to use gas to flush the Branch Davidians out peacefully, but a series of fires broke out and quickly spread, killing the vast majority of the occupants inside, including many young children.

Naturally, controversy spread over how the siege ended; for example, while most believe the Branch Davidians intentionally started the fires as part of a mass suicide, others insist it was the fault of the ATF. Debate also raged over whether the government could have and should have made different decisions to defuse the situation. As Alan Stone put it in a study of the siege,

"The tactical arm of federal law enforcement may conventionally think of the other side as a band of criminals or as a military force or, generically, as the aggressor. But the Branch Davidians were an unconventional group in an exalted, disturbed, and desperate state of mind. They were devoted to David Koresh as the Lamb of God. They were willing to die defending themselves in an apocalyptic ending and, in the alternative, to kill themselves and their children. However, these were neither psychiatrically depressed, suicidal people nor cold-blooded killers. They were ready to risk death as a test of their faith. The psychology of such behavior—together with its religious significance for the Branch Davidians—was mistakenly evaluated, if not simply ignored, by those responsible for the FBI strategy of 'tightening the noose'. The overwhelming show of force was not working in the way the tacticians supposed. It did not provoke the Branch Davidians to surrender, but it may have provoked David Koresh to order the mass-suicide." In 1999, a report prepared by the federal government itself concluded, "The violent tendencies of dangerous cults can be classified into two general categories—defensive violence and offensive violence. Defensive violence is utilized by cults to defend a compound or enclave that was created specifically to eliminate most contact with the dominant culture. The 1993 clash in Waco, Texas at the Branch Davidian complex is an illustration of such defensive violence. History has shown that groups that seek to withdraw from the dominant culture seldom act on their beliefs that the endtime has come unless provoked."

No matter which side people came down on, the violent confrontation embarrassed government officials, and Dick Morris, an advisor of Clinton's, even claimed that Attorney General Janet Reno only kept her job after Waco by threatening to pin the blame on the president: "[H]e went into a meeting with her, and he told me that she begged and pleaded, saying that . . . she didn't want to be fired because if she were fired it would look like he was firing her over Waco. And I knew that what that meant was that she would tell the truth about what happened in Waco. Now, to be fair, that's my supposition. I don't know what went on in Waco, but that was the cause. But I do know that she told him that if you fire me, I'm going to talk about Waco."

A picture of the Waco siege

   While the world watched in horror as the Branch Davidian Compound went up in smoke on April 19, 1993, no one was aware that there was a man standing in the shadows who would bring about another conflagration just two short years later. Timothy McVeigh, the product of an unloving, broken home, was a self-professed "survivalist" and a student of such books as *The Turner Diaries*, a novel raving against the United States and urging others to overthrow its government.

McVeigh

Although McVeigh held these sentiments from an early age, he still joined America's armed forces. In fact, he met Terry Nichols and Michael Fortier while in basic training in Georgia, and they had remained close throughout their time in the military, including serving together again at Fort Riley, Kansas. Prosecutor Joseph Hartzler summed up the relationships between the men: "Timothy McVeigh grew up in upstate New York; and after high school, he joined the Army. He first went to Fort Benning in Georgia, and that's where he met Terry Nichols. They served in Fort Benning in the same platoon. After he and Nichols completed their basic training at Fort Benning, they were both sent to Fort Riley, in Kansas. They became friends, in part because they both shared a distaste for the federal government. McVeigh's dislike for the federal government was revealed while he was still in the Army. Even at that early time in his life, he expressed an enthusiasm for this book *The Turner Diaries*. ... It follows the exploits of a group of well-armed men and women who call themselves 'patriots,' and they seek to overthrow the federal government by use of force and violence. In the book they make a fertilizer bomb in the back of a truck and they detonate it in front of a federal building in downtown Washington, D.C., during business hours and they kill hundreds of people. Friends, acquaintances, and family members of McVeigh will testify that he carried the book with him, gave copies to them, urged them to read this book."

While Nichols had left the Army in 1989, McVeigh stayed in and spent four months in the Persian Gulf. He also took a month of training for Special Forces, thinking he might make the Army his career, but his zeal waned and he left the service in December 1991. At that point, McVeigh moved in with his father in Buffalo and got a job with a security company that was proud to hire a man who had served his country.

Nichols

Fortier

Hiring a former veteran may have pleased the company, but McVeigh was becoming less proud of his service, and of his country. He became increasingly depressed and obsessed with

American politics, especially over what he saw as government incursions on his freedom. Over time, he began writing increasingly angry letters to politicians in his district, protesting everything from meatpacking practices to laws concerning carrying mace. For instance, in February 1992 he wrote to Congressman John LaFalce, "Recently, I saw an article in the Buffalo News that detailed a man's arrest; one of the charges being 'possession of a noxious substance' (CS gas). This struck my curiousity (sic), so I went to the New York State Penal Law. Sure enough, section 270 prohibits possession of any noxious substance, and included in section 265 is a ban on the use of 'stun guns'. Now I am a male, and fully capable of defending myself, but how about a female? I strongly believe in a God-given right to self-defense. Should any other person or a governing body be able to tell a person that he/she cannot save their own life, because it would be a violation of the law? In this case, which is more important: faced with a rapist/murderer, would you pick a.) die, a law abiding citizen or b.) live, and go to jail? It is a lie if we tell ourselves that the police can protect us everywhere, at all times. I am in shock that a law exists which denies a woman's right to self-defense. Firearms restrictions are bad enough, but now a woman can't even carry mace in her purse?!?!"

McVeigh also pressed his friends to share his ideas, including encouraging them to read *The Turner Diaries*. In the summer of 1992, he traveled to Michigan and stayed with Terry Nichols, who had also become disenchanted with the American government and had even gone so far as to renounce his citizenship, writing, "I am no longer a citizen of the corrupt political corporate state of Michigan and the United States of America." Together, the men followed the story of the FBI's raid on the home of survivalist and white separatist Randy Weaver in Ruby Ridge, Idaho in August 1992. Several people were killed during the raid, including Weaver's wife and teenage son. Weaver finally surrendered, but the government's reputation was severely tarnished and men like McVeigh were incensed.

Now thoroughly in the throes of the survivalist movement, McVeigh moved to Lockport, New York. He got a job with another security company but did not stay with it long, leaving in January 1993 to sell guns around the country. One gun collector later recalled to investigators how obsessed McVeigh was with *The Turner Diaries*: "He carried that book all the time. He sold it at the shows. He'd have a few copies in the cargo pocket of his cammies. They were supposed to be $10, but he'd sell them for $5. It was like he was looking for converts...He could make 10 friends at a show, just by his manner and demeanor. He's polite, he doesn't interrupt."

In the process, McVeigh met a fellow gun enthusiast named Roger Moore. The two discussed the ATF's February 28 raid in Waco and agreed that the government was becoming much too powerful. Angry, McVeigh decided to go to Texas and see things for himself.

Michelle Rausch was a journalism student at Southern Methodist University when she heard about the standoff in Waco, and she decided to head out to the compound to see for herself what was happening. By doing so, she became the one human connection between two historic events.

She later testified, "I was writing for the school paper and had kind of been following the Waco standoff, and I knew there was another angle to the story, and I wanted to find what that angle was. … So I took it upon myself during my spring break to travel to Waco to find what other angle to the, quote, 'Davidian standoff' there might be. … This is how I found Mr. McVeigh, when I walked up on the hill. He was sitting on the hood of his car with some bumper stickers that were for sale. … One of them I recall -- I can't see them clearly in this picture -- but Fear the Government that Fears Your Gun, Politicians Love Gun Control. … I told him who I was and I was doing a story for my school paper and asked him why he was there. … He said he just come in response to the standoff and that he -- he went on to say that he was opposed to how they handled the initial raid, that he thought it would be more appropriate had just the local sheriff gone down and issued an arrest warrant. … He had a lot of views that he shared with me, which is -- as a writer and a journalist, I enjoyed speaking with him to write about his views in my article."

Later, Rausch was asked to share with the court some of the quotes from McVeigh that she used in her article. "The first quote: I think if the sheriff served the warrant, it would all be okay. They're not tactical at all. They're government employees. This was in reference to the ATF. Next one: It seems like the ATF just wants a chance to play with their toys, paid for by government money. The next direct quote: The government is afraid of the guns people have because they have to have control of the people at all times. Once you take away the guns, you can do anything to the people. You give them an inch and they take a mile. I believe we are slowly turning into a socialist government. He said, The government is continually growing bigger and more powerful, and the people need to prepare to defend themselves against government control."

Rausch concluded her remarks by telling the court, "McVeigh said a sheriff should have served the warrant to Koresh without involving the ATF. Although McVeigh said he is sorry for those killed and injured, he said the ATF had no business being there in the first place. McVeigh said those in the ATF were merely pawns working under the control of government orders. The government thinks it has to spend taxpayer dollars on something, McVeigh said, adding that they saw this as an opportunity and seized it. McVeigh said he believes the government is greatly at fault in Waco and has broken constitutional laws. He quoted the U.S. Constitution and said U.S. armed forces should not be used against civilians, yet they were used against Koresh and his followers. McVeigh said he does not believe the Brady Bill is a solution or an adequate attempt at a compromise. McVeigh said the Koresh standoff is only the beginning and that people should watch the government's role and heed any warning signs."

McVeigh did not remain in Texas long during the siege. Instead, he traveled again to Michigan to visit Nichols, and the two men watched the final days of the Waco stand-off unfold on television, including the tragic April 19 raid on the building where the Branch Davidians were holed-up. When fires broke out inside, the two men joined many others in the country in believing the government was ultimately responsible.

Chapter 2: Fertilizer Fuel-Based Bomb

"As his hatred of the government grew, so did his interest in a knowledge of explosives. You'll hear that he and Terry Nichols had experimented with small explosives on Nichols' farm in Michigan. Later our evidence will prove that McVeigh graduated to larger bombs, and you'll hear about an incident that occurred just one year before the bombing in a desert in Arizona where he made and detonated a pipe bomb. He placed it near a large boulder in the desert, and he ran away as the pipe bomb exploded and cracked the boulder. You will see that he also educated himself about how to build bombs, particularly truck bombs, using ammonium nitrate fertilizer and some sort of fuel oil. And we'll explain to you how you can make a bomb from fertilizer and fuel oil, and of course that's consistent with the type of destructive device that was used in Oklahoma City…he also obtained what was really a cookbook on how to make bombs. He ordered the book through the mail, we will show you; and the book is called Home Made C4. C4 is a type explosive. Some of you with military background know that. This book provides essentially a step-by-step recipe as to how to put together your own fertilizer fuel-based bomb."
– Joseph Hartzler, prosecutor in the case against McVeigh

"A man with nothing left to lose is a very dangerous man and his energy/anger can be focused toward a common/righteous goal. What I'm asking you to do, then, is sit back and be honest with yourself. Do you have kids/wife? Would you back out at the last minute to care for the family? Are you interested in keeping your firearms for their current/future monetary value, or would you drag that '06 through rock, swamp and cactus...to get off the needed shot? In short, I'm not looking for talkers, I'm looking for fighters...And if you are a fed, think twice. Think twice about the Constitution you are supposedly enforcing (isn't "enforcing freedom" an oxymoron?) and think twice about catching us with our guard down – you will lose just like Degan did – and your family will lose." – A letter written by McVeigh to Steve Colbern, one of his customers

Not surprisingly, Waco only fueled the two men's hatred of the government, and shortly thereafter, while traveling with his gun business to Kingman, Arizona, McVeigh met up again with Fortier. McVeigh began to talk to Fortier about his belief that it was time to overthrow the government by any means necessary, and he introduced Fortier to *The Turner Diaries*. Fortier in turn introduced McVeigh to marijuana and crystal meth.

Together, the two discussed forming a militia group, and McVeigh remained in Kingman for the rest of the summer, working as a security guard. According to Fortier, "Somewhere along the line at one of the gun shows, he found a tape called, 'Waco, The Big Lie,' which we viewed at my house. We discussed the tape. Mostly we just rehashed the same old discussion over and over again. [He said those people were] Murdered and that there was a cover-up, that somebody should be held accountable."

In March 1994, McVeigh met with Andreas Strassmeir, head of a private militia based at Elohim City, a private community in Oklahoma founded by right-wing extremists. The two men stayed in touch, even while McVeigh continued to live in Kingman. By this time, McVeigh had become increasingly militant in his attitude toward the government; he created a bunker around his home in Arizona, began making and testing bombs, and on March 16, 1994, he renounced his citizenship.

A few months later, in July, McVeigh and Fortier started stealing regularly from the local National Guard Armory. Fortier later admitted, "One day at work Tim approached me and said that he had been noticing on his way to work each morning that there was a buildup happening at the local National Guard armory. He said over a period of days there is just more and more vehicles being parked in the back area. He asked me if I wanted to go with him one night to go check it out, which I did in the middle of the night. Me and Tim went and jumped the back fence, looked in the back of all the vehicles, and we looked at the bumper numbers. We just scouted around to see if there was any evidence of UN activity. ... We were peeking in the back of the trucks. They were all empty. As we were leaving, I came across some . . . a couple shovels, a couple picks, and two axes, which we stole. They were located on the undercarriage of a Humvee, which is like a Jeep. We had to hide underneath the Jeep because there was a diesel getting off the highway, and its lights flashed across the National Guard armory's yard, and we did not want to be seen, so we slid underneath the Jeeps; and that's when I noticed that they were there. And we just, on the spur of the moment, decided to take them."

Even stranger, McVeigh and Fortier began sneaking into the famous government site known as Area 51 in Roswell, New Mexico. However, they were not looking for aliens but for signs the government was getting ready to impose martial law.

In September 1994, McVeigh left Oklahoma and visited Gulfport, Mississippi. McVeigh seemed to have heard a rumor that there were United Nations troops massing along the Mississippi coast, so he went to see for himself if there was evidence for this. Though he found none, that did nothing to allay his fears of a One World Government. In fact, later that month, McVeigh went to Elohim City to participate in military exercises with the militia there.

It was during his weekend at Elohim City that McVeigh began to openly discuss a plan to detonate a large bomb at the Murrah Federal Building in Oklahoma City. According to Prosecutor Joseph Hartzler, "Over time McVeigh's anger and hatred of the government kept growing; and in the late summer of 1994...he decided that he had had enough. He told friends that he was done distributing antigovernment propaganda and talking about the coming revolution. He said it was time to take action, and the action he wanted to take was something dramatic, something that would shake up America, he said, and would cause ordinary citizens, he thought, to engage in a violent revolution against their democratically elected government.... The action he selected was the bombing, and the building he selected was the federal building in

Oklahoma City. … And he offered two reasons for bombing -- or for selecting that particular building; first he thought that the ATF agents, whom he blamed for the Waco tragedy, had their offices in that building. …second, he described that building as, quote, 'an easy target.' It was conveniently located just south of Kansas and it had easy access. It was just a matter of blocks off of an interstate highway, Interstate 35 through Oklahoma City traveling north; and the building is designed is such that you can drive a truck up, there is an indentation at the sidewalk in front of the building. You can drive a truck right up and park a truck right there in front of the building, right there in front of the plate glass windows…of the day-care center."

After leaving Elohim City, McVeigh traveled to Herington, Kansas, where he rented a storage unit, and on September 30, he bought a ton of ammonium nitrate, a fertilizer that he would later use to make the bomb for the Murrah Building. A few days later, on October 3, McVeigh stole dynamite and blasting caps from a nearby quarry.

In October, McVeigh returned to Michigan to see Nichols for a bit before they both headed back to Elohim City. From that time forward, McVeigh began using the alias Tim Tuttle to buy up large quantities of nitromethane, a powerful chemical used as a fuel in drag racing, among other things. It is also an important ingredient for making explosives and at the time was available in larger hobby shops because it was also used by radio controlled vehicle hobbyists.

During mid-October, McVeigh and Nichols spent two weeks in Arizona before returning to McPherson and purchasing another ton of fertilizer. Fortier later testified, "We got into a storage locker that they had rented, and Tim showed me some explosives that were inside it. I don't recall exactly the explosives I seen that night. What I recall, Tim had a flashlight, and the main part of the beam was shining on the box; and it had a -- and one of those orange triangles or yellow triangles -- not a triangle. Excuse me -- a diamond that says 'explosives.' That's what I remember seeing mostly. Tim was reaching into the box and showing me some explosives, but I don't remember exactly what it was he showed me. …he was squatted down before a blanket that was covering some items that appeared to be more of the boxes containing explosives. I could estimate there were about three high, two and two deep. That would be about 12 boxes."

On October 20, McVeigh and Nichols made their first trip to the building they would soon target for destruction. They stopped their car in front of the Murrah Federal Building and then used a watch to time how far away McVeigh could get before the bomb went off. The next day, McVeigh went to Dallas and, disguised as a biker, bought $3,000 worth of nitromethane. He and Nichols then joined Fortier in Kingman, where the two men devoted themselves to perfecting their explosive mixture for maximum damage. Fortier's wife, Lori, later testified about one of these experiments: "One day me and Michael went over to Tim's house in Golden Valley, and he was in the process of finishing making a pipe bomb; and he asked us to go up in the mountains and blow it off with him. …it was approximately a foot, foot and a half long, a couple inches in diameter, and it was made up of gun powder. And when we got there, he was putting the cap on it, on the end of it. … We drove to an area between Golden Valley and Laughlin, Nevada. It's a mountain range called Union Pass, and we walked up about a mile, maybe 2 miles into the mountains. … We walked into the mountains, and Tim put it under a boulder and set it off. … [There was] A big cloud of smoke, and Tim and Mike went up there to look at what happened to the boulder, and it split in half."

Building this bomb was expensive work, and McVeigh and Nichols soon realized that they would have to come up with some way to finance their plot. Therefore, in November 1994, they found some men willing to break into a house and steal a number of valuable items that they then sold. The following month, McVeigh himself committed a number of robberies.

About this time, McVeigh took Fortier to the Federal Building in Oklahoma City to show him the target he had chosen. Fortier explained, "Well, we left Amarillo, and we were driving up to Kansas; and as we passed through Oklahoma City, Tim got off the highway saying he wanted to show me the building. … We drove by the back of the building first…I'm speaking of the federal building Tim was pointing out. …Tim asked me if I thought that a truck of the size he was speaking of would fit in the -- I'm not sure what it -- it looks like a commercial -- like a drop-off zone or just a little pull-in that's in front of the building. And I said, 'Yeah, you could probably fit three trucks in the front there.' And he drove further on, and then we turned into an alley, and he pointed out a spot where he was going to park his vehicle there. … He said he was thinking of doing one of two things: One being Terry would follow him down in the morning, that he was planning this, and wait for him in this parking spot, or that they would drop a vehicle off there a couple days earlier and then Tim would just drive the truck down, himself, and then run to the car and get in it and drive away. …I asked Tim why he wouldn't park closer…. And he said he didn't want to do that because he wanted to have a building between him and the blast."

Once they were back in Kansas, McVeigh and Nichols continued to perfect their plans for the attack, and in February 1995, they moved their bomb making material twice, first to a storage unit McVeigh rented in Herington, Kansas, and then to Fortier's home in Arizona. By this time, Strassmeir and a man named Dennis Mahon had also become interested in possibly bombing some large government facility in Oklahoma City. However, they were not as discreet as McVeigh was, so they eventually came to the attention of ATF agent Carole Howe. After a number of discussions between the ATF, the FBI, and the Attorney's General's office, the ATF decided not to raid Elohim City but to wait for more information. It is possible if not likely that the agency's decision was influenced by the previous disaster in Waco.

In March, just a month before the attack, Nichols began having second thoughts. He decided that while he was comfortable with helping McVeigh develop the bomb, he did not want to be around when McVeigh used it. McVeigh was disappointed but still went forward with his plan. According to Lori Fortier, "I was at the house, and he came and asked if he could use the typewriter; and I let him take it for a couple days. He brought it back a few days after that; and when he brought it back, he asked if he could use the iron, because he had something to laminate. And I told him no because I didn't want him to ruin our iron. So I took what it was that he had and I laminated it for him. It was a false driver's license. It was white. It had like a blue strip across the top, and Tim had put his picture on there. And it was like the false name of Robert Kling. I believe it was a North Dakota license. ... We made a joke about, like Star Trek and Klingon. It was something that was from Star Trek, so we made a joke about the name."

On April 5, McVeigh called someone in Elohim City. This person later became known as John Doe #2, but they have never been identified. Meanwhile, around this time, Fortier also decided to back out of the plan. As Lori later recounted in her testimony, "It was the first week of April, and me and Michael went to the Imperial Motel. Michael had a book that Tim had loaned him. Tim said that he wanted Michael to read the book, and Mike was giving the book back to him. We were scared of Tim, so Mike brought his gun with him at that time…we weren't really friends anymore, and we were really scared of him. …he had told us everything about this, and we wanted out; and we thought he'd kill us because he had told us about it. [We were there] just a few minutes. We walked in, gave him the book, and we left."

Undeterred, McVeigh remained in Kingman for the next week, and at one point he visited a strip club in nearby Tulsa with Strassmeir and Michael Brescia. The government later investigated videotape from that night, and the investigation discovered that McVeigh had ominously told one dancer, "On April 19, you'll remember me for the rest of my life."

Chapter 3: A Catastrophic Explosion

"ATF, all you tyrannical people will swing in the wind one day for your treasonous actions against the Constitution of the United States. Remember the Nuremberg War Trials." – Excerpt from a letter written by McVeigh to the ATF shortly before the attack

"At 9:02 that morning…a catastrophic explosion ripped the air in downtown Oklahoma City. It instantaneously demolished the entire front of the Murrah Building…dismembered people inside, and it destroyed, forever, scores and scores and scores of lives, lives of innocent Americans…All the children I mentioned earlier, all of them died, and more; dozens and dozens of other men, women, children, cousins, loved ones, grandparents, grandchildren, ordinary Americans going about their business. And the only reason they died, the only reason that they are no longer with us, no longer with their loved ones, is that they were in a building owned by a government that Timothy McVeigh so hated that with premeditated intent and a well-designed plan that he had developed over months and months before the bombing, he chose to take their innocent lives to serve his twisted purpose. In plain, simple language, it was an act of terror, violence, intend -- intended to serve selfish political purpose. The man who committed this act is sitting in this courtroom behind me, and he's the one that committed those murders. After he did so, he fled the scene; and he avoided even damaging his eardrums, because he had earplugs with him." – Joseph Hartzler, prosecutor in the case against McVeigh

On April 13, McVeigh made yet another visit to Oklahoma City, this time to find a place where he could leave his car after the attack. He also visited his storage shed in Herington and verified that he had all the supplies he needed. The next day, he bought a 1977 Mercury Marquis and called to reserve a Ryder truck. He met Terry Nichols at nearby Geary Lake to get some more money and then checked into the Dreamland Motel in Junction City.

On April 16, he met Nichols in Herington and the two men drove to Oklahoma City. McVeigh left his Marquis near the Murrah building and Nichols drove him back to Kansas.

The following day, McVeigh picked up his reserved Ryder truck and drove it back to the Dreamland Motel, where he was still staying. Early on the morning of the 18th, he drove the truck to his storage unit, where Nichols came to meet him, and together the two men loaded the bags of fertilizer and the drums of nitromethane into the back of the truck. Lori Fortier subsequently testified about a conversation they had once had about the way McVeigh would set up the bomb in the truck: "He wasn't sure whether he was going to drill holes into the cab of the truck, or if the truck had windows, he was going to like just put them through the windows. The fuse. There would be two separate fuses. ... He used the term 'shape charge.' ... By drawing the barrels in the truck, he formed them in a triangle shape with the biggest part of the triangle would be facing the building to get the most...impact.... He said that he and Terry would do it together; that Terry would mix the bomb. ... He had a book that had the different detonation ratios, I guess you'd call it, of different types of explosives."

Next, the two men drove to Geary Lake, where they could mix the explosive chemicals without being watched. From there, McVeigh drove alone to Ponca City, Oklahoma, where he parked his truck and slept for the night.

McVeigh awoke early on the morning of April 19 and left Ponca City around 7:00 a.m., headed for Oklahoma City and his massive attack. That same morning, as prosecutor Joseph Hartzler pointed out, parents were dropping off children at the daycare center inside the Murrah Federal Building: "When [Helena Garrett] turned to leave to go to her work, Tevin, as so often, often happens with small children, cried and clung to her; and then, as you see with children so frequently, they try to help each other. Little -- one of the little Coverdale boys -- there were two of them, Elijah and Aaron. The youngest one was two and a half. Elijah came up to Tevin and patted him on the back and comforted him as his mother left. As Helena Garrett left the Murrah Federal Building to go to work across the street, she could look back up at the building; and there was a wall of plate glass windows on the second floor. You can look through those windows and see into the day-care center; and the children would run up to those windows and press their hands and faces to those windows to say goodbye to their parents. And standing on the sidewalk, it was almost as though you can reach up and touch the children there on the second floor. But none of the parents of any of the children that I just mentioned ever touched those children again while they were still alive."

McVeigh got into town around 8:50 and drove straight for the Murrah Federal Building. He drove up NW 5th Street and lit the two fuses for his bomb. He then parked his truck in front of the building, locked it, and walked away from the site to his getaway car. Two minutes later, at exactly 9:02 a.m., the truck exploded.

An aerial view of the building

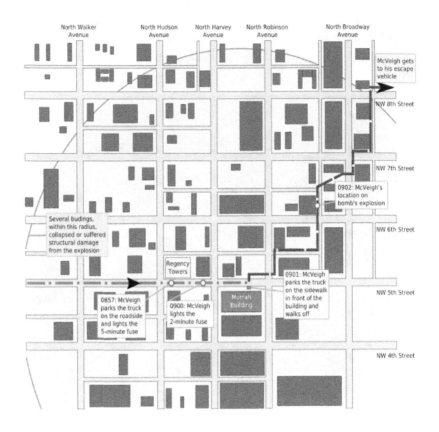

A map of the area and the route McVeigh took to get away

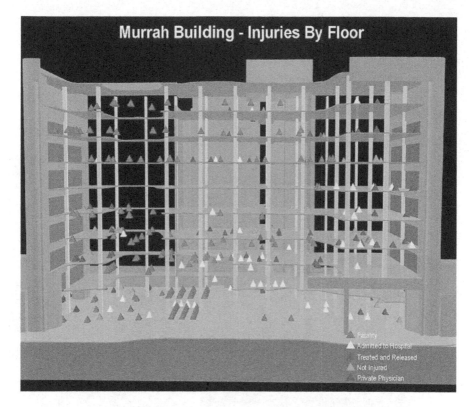

Murrah Building - Injuries By Floor

Fatality
Admitted to Hospital
Treated and Released
Not Injured
Private Physician

A graphic indicating the location of the dead and injured

The day care center in the Murrah Federal Building was nearest to where McVeigh parked the truck, so most of the children there were killed instantly. When he was later asked if he and McVeigh ever discussed the inevitable deaths that would result, Fortier answered, "I asked him about that... I said, 'What about all the people?' And he explained to me, using the terms from the movie 'Star Wars' -- he explained to me that he considered all those people to be as if they were the storm troopers in the movie 'Star Wars.' They may be individually innocent; but because they are part of the -- the evil empire, they were -- they were guilty by association." Apparently, McVeigh failed to explain how the children were guilty or why he chose to park the Ryder truck right in front of the daycare center.

Regardless, within a split second of the massive explosion, the rest of the building also began to collapse. One reporter who interviewed people at the building that day described the scene: "First the ceiling collapsed. Then the wires fell. Next the pipes sagged, broke and crashed down, crunching jagged shards of broken glass that covered every surface. A fog of white dust hung in the air. 'I've got to get out of here,' thought Brian Espe, hunkered down beneath a massive conference table on the fifth floor of the federal building moments after a car bomb ripped its guts out and peeled off the north wall. 'But I've got to be very careful.' Espe, 57, an Agriculture Department veterinarian, picked himself up gingerly from the rubble and looked around. He noticed that some USDA offices, like his conference room, had been turned upside down as if by a cyclone, but most of the fifth floor was simply obliterated: 'the north side of the building disappeared,' Espe said. 'I could walk through a wall and step into space.' Fortunately, he was on the south side, far from the explosion but still teetering on the edge of oblivion."

Pictures of the building taken a week later by FEMA

Pictures of the extent of the damage taken by FEMA

For each life that the bomb took that morning, it changed 100 others. 48 year old James Hargrave, who worked on the third floor in the Office of the Inspector General of the Department of Health and Human Services, told the *New York Times*, "I was on the phone and did not hear any explosion, just felt things falling on my head. And I really thought it was an earthquake or something similar. When I stood, I was completely free; it just kind of all fell around me. And I searched for the people in my office. The strange thing was, it was like I was the only person alive. There was no screaming, no moaning, no hissing from gas lines, none of the things you so normally see on a TV show. It was almost silent. I found most of the people in my office, and we dug them out. And there didn't seem to be anyone that was hurt severely, and our first inclination was to get out. And I said, 'Well, is anybody hurt?' And this other voice said: 'Yes, I'm hurt. Could you help me?' And we found this guy that was in our office, and we kind of start digging him out. And we ask him, 'Who are you?' And he said that he was from the seventh floor. ... We jerked them down, tied them into a knot, these huge curtains that went from ceiling to floor, and they kind of used it as a hammock and a rope at the same time. They kind of laid on it and kind of just scooted down the side of the building."

Hargrave then made a grim observation, the result of a detachment caused by a combination of shock and sorrow: "The only bad thing about this story, because all of our people are not hurt seriously, was the one young lady has an infant in the day-care center.... And when you get out, we had to actually -- the level we got out on the ground is the day-care playground. So we had to walk through that playground, and then we found out later that most of the babies and young children had died." In fact, some of the children in the center did survive and, seeing their teachers and friends dead around them, ran from the area looking for the only people they thought might be able to help them. Calvin Johnson, a janitor at an Oklahoma hotel, recalled, "I was coming out of the courthouse when I was thrown against the building wall. Initially I saw glass falling and two cars in the middle of the street, and I thought there had been a car wreck. Then I saw the smoke and realized what had happened. I ran toward the Federal building, a block away. I wasn't concerned about myself, because I was on my feet. I wanted to see if there was something I could do for someone else. There were people running past me, all bloody, and I saw a kid running along -- he was 2 or 3 years old, a little black kid. I think he thought I was his father. He was hollering: 'Dad! Dad!' I picked him up and carried him to the other side of the street, to the corner where the courthouse is. By this time, the streets were loaded with people running from every side. I don't have any idea how he is, or how his family is. I don't remember what he was wearing, and if somebody was to hand him to me now, I wouldn't know if it was him or not."

Fortunately, some parents were able to find their children, even in the minutes after the bombing. Ondre King worked across the street from the Murrah Federal Building and had a 2 year old daughter in the daycare center. The day after the attack, she said, "She was already outside by the time I got there. She was just drenched with blood. … And there was a whole bunch of ambulances and police out there. And I seen all that black smoke, and it looked like there was a car on fire. And when we got to the hospital at like 9:30, then she started hollering and crying, because they started messing with her. And they had to sedate her to work with her. And I thought, 'Oh, my God, my baby's finger was blown off, and they had to sew it back on.' I think the glass, it hurt, because she got stitches all on the rim of her ears, and on the back of her ears. Then she got I don't know how many stitches on her thumb. That was cut pretty deep, on the left hand. And she has stitches on her left thigh. And she has a few scratches on her face and a few scratches on her cheek and on her back. Her back is pretty bruised. And she still has glass and stuff in her hair. I'm still picking glass and stuff out of my hair. I think they're kind of embedded in my scalp; I'm scared to scratch it."

While it was the children's injuries and deaths that were the most heart wrenching, most of those harmed that day were adults. Wanda Webster was 65 and worked for the Office of Native American Programs of the Department of Housing and Urban Development in the building. She told reporters, "The blast hit, and it threw me up against a wall, and another wall collapsed on top of me. It was like the end of the world when the blast hit, this tremendous noise and pressure against you. And I could see everything disintegrating. I had no sense of direction, but I dug myself out of the rubble. I don't know how long it took, I was so disoriented. But I was in a pocket; our ceiling didn't collapse. And when I finally did remove the rubble and stand up, there was nothing there. You didn't know where you were. There were two other workers and myself. We started crawling toward some light. But then we realized we were crawling toward the edge of the window that had blown out, and we turned around and were able to get to the only remaining staircase. And we walked out of the building."

Not everyone injured was trapped in the rubble. Auditor Richard Slay explained, "I arrived at just about 9 o'clock and walked…right over to the elevators, punched the 'up' button. … As soon as the doors opened, the air in the elevator shaft started whooshing out. There must have been little pebbles and dirt in the elevator shaft getting sucked up. It pelted my right hand and my right arm, where I was just wearing a button-down shirt -- I had it rolled up. The blast of air came first, and then the explosion. I immediately dropped to the ground and kind of turned away from the elevator shaft, because I felt certain that there would be a fireball coming out there. I didn't want to get blasted in the face. But the fireball never came. And the building just started sliding into the street. I could just hear it. And right above me, all around me, the first thing, the most immediate thing, was the redwood ceiling was falling. But it never touched me. And then some air ducts, that stuff was falling down. And other metal, aluminum-type sheeting stuff was falling. But none of it was hitting me. That was really miraculous. Then it all just kind of stopped, and it got very quiet."

Slay stood there for a few minutes before he reacted: "My first thought was, 'I'll just stay here until some rescue workers come.' Then I started smelling smoke, and that started changing my thinking a little bit. I had started calling out to see if there were survivors: 'Is anyone here?' I didn't get any responses. I heard some groans. It took a while to even start hearing groans…Then I noticed a white cloud moving in. I had never smelled that stuff before. It was acrid. I thought it must have been gas from the explosion…I started moving. I was walking over mounds of rubble. Then I heard a lady say, 'I think I have an exit here.' She opened a door. There was a lot of light coming in, but there was so much rubble I told her I didn't think we wanted to walk through all that mess. With the light, I could see the double doors to the loading dock. I said, 'Let's go this way.' Outside I looked east, and it was just a nightmare. The cars were on fire, and there were plumes of smoke everywhere. So we went west across the street to the Catholic rectory. By this time, the lady I was with just collapsed. She just crumpled to the ground."

Fire trucks, ambulances and other vehicles quickly arrived on the scene. Paramedic John Grifith remembered, "It's like they dumped it in with a dump truck. Imagine taking an office and putting it in a blender and turning it on. Everything was upside down — computers, keyboards." He told the story of one woman he was trying to rescue when the workers were ordered from the building due to fears of further collapse. The woman begged Grifith not to leave her. "I said, 'I don't want to, but they're making me.' I put myself in her place, and thought how terribly alone." When he got back to her 45 minutes later, "She kept asking over and over if we would ever get her out. I told her she was just having a bad hair day and they were going to dock her for laying down on the job." In the wake of the attacks, firefighter Mike Roberts told reporters, "We've been digging on this lady for the last hour. She's still alive. I gave her water. I said, 'We're going to get you out.' She said, 'Do you think you can?' I said, 'Yeah." Finally, five hours later, the woman was carried out. According to the article, "As she was loaded into the ambulance, a chaplain approached Grifith. Standing in the pouring rain with the shell of the federal building behind them, they closed their eyes, bowed their heads and prayed."

A news service article reported, "The blast occurred at the start of a work day, as parents dropped off their youngsters at the day-care center in the federal building. Before the smoke cleared, emergency worker Heather Taylor had put tags on the toes of at least 12 children. Assistant Fire Chief Jon Hansen described the first 30 minutes after the bombing as 'pure mayhem.' Streets were choked with walking wounded, emergency crews and well-meaning citizens. Some people, apparently driving near the federal building at the time of the blast, appeared to have been killed in their cars. Inside the federal building, survivors were screaming and crying, Hansen said, 'We're having to crawl over victims to try and reach the living, and often all we can do is hold their hand.' ... By noon, the only sounds rescuers in the federal building could hear were made by other rescue workers, said Officer Adrian Neal of the Edmond Police Department. By 1:30 p.m., many medical personnel were sent home."

A picture of rescue workers receiving communion

A picture of rescue efforts taken on April 21

Pictures of search and rescue and salvage operations

Chapter 4: 75 Minutes Later

"Approximately 75 minutes later, about 75 miles north of Oklahoma City, the exact distance from Oklahoma City that you could drive in that time if you had been at the scene of the crime, the exact distance...you would reach between the time of the bombing and the time he was arrested if you were driving at normal speed limit. And on his clothing, an FBI chemist later found residue of explosives, undetonated explosives, not the kind of residue that would detonate in the course of the explosion but the kind of explosives you would have on your clothing if you had made the bomb.... And the T-shirt he was wearing virtually broadcast his intention. On its front was the image of Abraham Lincoln; and beneath the image was a phrase about tyrants, which is a phrase that John Wilkes Booth shouted in Ford's Theater to the audience when he murdered President Lincoln. And on the back of the T-shirt that McVeigh was wearing on that morning...was this phrase: It said, 'The tree of liberty must be refreshed from time to time with the blood of patriots and tyrants.' And above those words was the image of a tree...the tree on the T-shirt bears a depiction of droplets of scarlet-red blood." – Joseph Hartzler, prosecutor in the case against McVeigh

"I am sorry these people had to lose their lives. But that's the nature of the beast. It's understood going in what the human toll will be." – Timothy McVeigh

While people were responding to the explosion, McVeigh was driving down the highway, intent on making his escape. However, he had made a critical error, one that would ultimately bring him to justice. State Trooper Charles Hanger explained in his testimony, "I was northbound on the interstate in the left-hand lane when I came upon a vehicle which was a yellow 1977 Mercury Marquis, four-door. It had a primer spot on the left rear quarter panel. And I started around that vehicle in the left lane, it was in the right lane traveling north, I observed that it was not displaying a tag on the rear bumper. I slowed down, fell in behind the vehicle, got in the same lane it was in. Initiated my emergency lights and signaled for it to pull over. It began slowing down and pulling over to the east side of the roadway, the shoulder. ... We met behind his car. About 3 or 4 feet south of the left rear corner of his car and off to the west 3 or 4 feet. And I told him why I'd stopped him."

McVeigh was polite and cooperative, but in the next few moments, his situation evolved from being issued a traffic ticket, or maybe just a warning, to being arrested on a felony. Hanger noted, "As he was going to his right rear pocket to retrieve his billfold, he had on a blue windbreaker-type jacket that was just slightly zipped, and when he went to his pocket, it tightened this jacket up somewhat; and I could see a bulge under his left arm, and I thought that that was a weapon under his arm. I looked at the driver's license and looked at him. Then I instructed him to take both hands, unzip his jacket, and to very slowly move his jacket back. He took both hands, he unzipped his jacket, and started slowly pulling it back; and just as he started doing that, he said, 'I have a gun.' I grabbed for the bulge, and I said, 'Put your hands up and turn around.' ... I removed my pistol from my holster and stuck it to the back of his head. I instructed him to walk to the trunk of his automobile."

McVeigh had to have been aware by this time that he was now in deep trouble. Still, he remained polite and cooperative in every way possible. According to Hanger, "He said, 'My weapon is loaded.' I said, 'So is mine.' I instructed him to put his hands on the trunk and to spread his feet. ... I then pulled back the jacket, removed the pistol from the holster it was in, and threw it on the shoulder of the roadway. ... He informed me that he also had another clip and a pouch on his belt. ... He told me that he also had a knife on his belt. ... I then patted him down and handcuffed him. ... I took him to the right front passenger seat of my unit, placed him in there and seat-belted him in. ... I placed [the gun and the knife] in the trunk of my unit. Also checked the weapon to see if it was loaded. Removed the clip from the bottom of the weapon, then I checked the chamber of the weapon and removed a round from that chamber. ... I asked him if he wanted me to tow the car or leave it at the roadside. And I explained to him the difference, that if I impound the car, I'll make a inventory of it and list his property for his protection, and if he leaves it at the roadside, it will be left at his own risk. He said, "Just leave it."

As a result, McVeigh was charged with "Transporting a loaded firearm in a motor vehicle, unlawfully carrying a weapon, failure to display a current number plate, which is a tag, on a motor vehicle and failure to maintain proof of security, which is liability insurance." Later that day, as McVeigh sat in his holding cell, President Clinton spoke to the American people:

> "The bombing in Oklahoma City was an attack on innocent children and defenseless citizens. It was an act of cowardice, and it was evil. The United States will not tolerate it. And I will not allow the people of this country to be intimidated by evil cowards. I have met with our team, which we assembled to deal with this bombing. And I have determined to take the following steps to assure the strongest response to this situation:

> "First, I have deployed a crisis management team under the leadership of the FBI, working with the Department of Justice, the Bureau of Alcohol, Tobacco and Firearms, military and local authorities. We are sending the world's finest investigators to solve these murders.

> "Second, I have declared an emergency in Oklahoma City. And at my direction, James Lee Witt, the Director of the Federal Emergency Management Agency, is now on his way there to make sure we do everything we can to help the people of Oklahoma deal with the tragedy.

> "Third, we are taking every precaution to reassure and to protect people who work in or live near other Federal facilities.

"Let there be no room for doubt: We will find the people who did this. When we do, justice will be swift, certain, and severe. These people are killers, and they must be treated like killers. Finally, let me say that I ask all Americans tonight to pray— to pray for the people who have lost their lives, to pray for the families and the friends of the dead and the wounded, to pray for the people of Oklahoma City. May God's grace be with them. Meanwhile, we will be about our work."

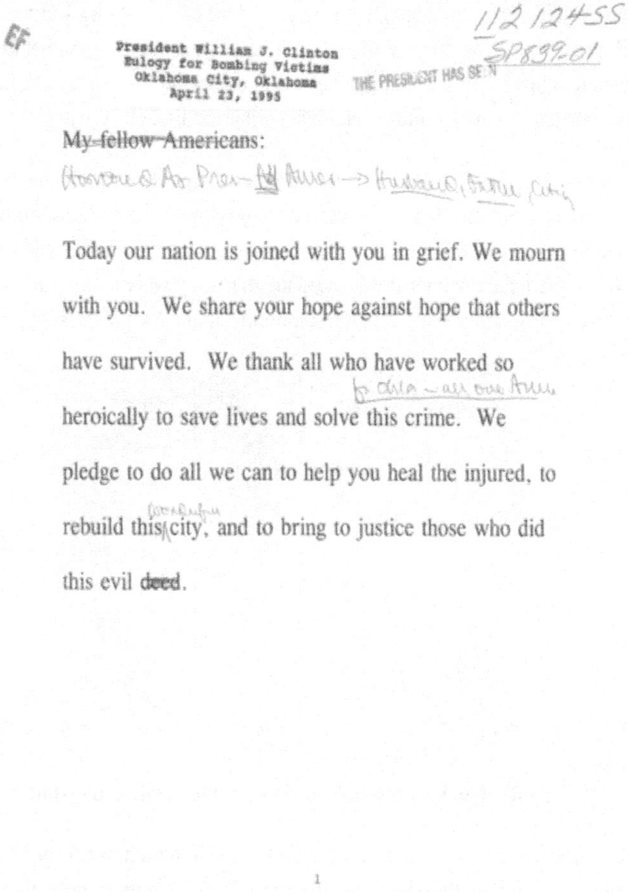

EF

11212455
SP839-01

President William J. Clinton
Eulogy for Bombing Victims
Oklahoma City, Oklahoma
April 23, 1995

THE PRESIDENT HAS SEEN

~~My fellow Americans:~~

(Honorable As Pres— 1st Amer — → Husband, Father City)

Today our nation is joined with you in grief. We mourn

with you. We share your hope against hope that others

have survived. We thank all who have worked so

to Okla — all our true

heroically to save lives and solve this crime. We

pledge to do all we can to help you heal the injured, to

(communities)

rebuild this city, and to bring to justice those who did

this evil ~~deed~~.

1

A picture of Clinton's personal notes for his address on the bombing

Furthermore, Clinton wrote to Frank Keating, the Governor of Oklahoma, assuring him, "I have declared an emergency under the Robert T. Stafford Disaster Relief and Emergency Assistance Act (the Stafford Act) for the city of Oklahoma City in the State of Oklahoma due to the explosion at the Federal courthouse in Oklahoma City on April 19, 1995 in the State of Oklahoma. I have authorized Federal relief and emergency assistance in the affected area."

By this time, Trooper Hanger had become aware of two critical pieces of evidence. The first was something he overheard: "I had heard Mrs. Moritz [the woman booking McVeigh] ask him who he wanted to list as next of kin. And he didn't say anything. And I heard her ask that same question again. He still didn't say anything. So I...got up from the chair that I was sitting in at the computer and walked up to the booking counter. ... And I said, 'Well, what about the address listed on the license?' I said, 'Who lives there?' ... He said that was a place that he had stayed; it was a -- belonged to a brother of a friend that he was in the military with. ... The last name was Nichols. At that particular time I couldn't remember what the first name was."

By this time, the police had circulated a sketch of a man they called "John Doe No. 1." The sketch was based on descriptions they had received from witnesses at the site. Ironically, one of his former co-workers had identified McVeigh as the suspect, and the police had issued a warrant for his arrest. When the federal authorities learned the man they were looking for was already in custody, they picked McVeigh up and transferred him to Tinker Air Force Base.

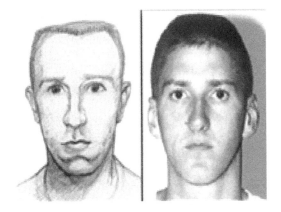

An FBI sketch of the suspect next to McVeigh's mugshot

That evening, Terry Nichols went to the police station in Herington and turned himself in and gave them permission to search his house. Shortly thereafter, Trooper Hanger discovered another critical piece of evidence: "On the morning of the 22d, which would be the next shift that I worked after completing my shift on the 19th, I'd went to work that day, and I made a search of the, visual search of the area of my car. I always look at the floorboards and the seats to see if anything that might have been left in there that could be used as a weapon. And while I was doing that, I looked in the right rear floorboard and there was a crumpled-up white business card laying in the floorboard. ... It says, 'Paulsen's Military Supply.' [On the back] In big capital letters it says, 'Dave,' and then in parentheses, it says '(TNT @ $5 a stick. Need more.)' Below that is a telephone number that says, '708-288-0128.' Below that in printing it says, 'Call after 1

May see if I can get some more.'"

Chapter 5: This Terrible Crime

Graffiti left by Rescue Team 5 in remembrance of the victims

"Each of the crimes has various elements. The Judge at the end of the case will instruct you on those elements. It's our burden to prove each of the elements for each of the counts. We will meet that burden. We will make your job easy. We will present ample evidence to convince you beyond any reasonable doubt that Timothy McVeigh is responsible for this terrible crime. You will hear evidence in this case that McVeigh liked to consider himself a patriot, someone who could start the second American Revolution. The literature that was in his car when he was arrested included some that quoted statements from the founding fathers and other people who played a part in the American Revolution, people like Patrick Henry and Samuel Adams. McVeigh isolated and took these statements out of context, and he did that to justify his anti-government violence. Well, ladies and gentlemen, the statements of our forefathers can never be televised to justify warfare against innocent children. Our forefathers didn't fight British women and children. They fought other soldiers. They fought them face to face, hand to hand. They didn't plant bombs and run away wearing earplugs" – Joseph Hartzler, prosecutor in the case against McVeigh

"I knew I wanted this before it happened. I knew my objective was state-assisted suicide and when it happens, it's in your face. You just did something you're trying to say should be illegal for medical personnel." – Timothy McVeigh

On April 27, 1995, the United States District Court for the Western District of Oklahoma heard the evidence against McVeigh, and at the end of that proceeding, the U.S. Attorney concluded, "You have heard evidence, Your Honor, more than sufficient to establish that during and relation to a crime of violence the Defendant used and carried a destructive device that is a bomb. Therefore, the presumption applies and should be detained. … Finally, Your Honor with respect to the safety of the community, the statute directs us to look at the nature of the offense and could not imagine a more heinous offense than this. The Defendant has shown a willingness to kill innocent children, law enforcement officers, and ordinary people going about their ordinary lives. No series of the conditions could reasonably assure his appearance or the safety of other persons in the community. For that reason, he should be detained." The next day, the United States Magistrate ordered McVeigh held without bail. Nichols, however, was not formally arrested until May 10.

A picture of McVeigh in custody

A picture of the Murrah Federal Building being demolished in May 1995

A few days after McVeigh's arraignment, on May 4, the search for bodies in the remains of the Murrah Federal Building ended. The next day, an Associated Press article reported that "firefighters found the remains of the last nine victims, Assistant Fire Chief Jon Hansen said. The grim discovery in the last 6- foot pile of unsearched rubble brought the death toll to 168 and came despite fears earlier in the week that some of the bodies would never be found. Among the sets of nearly two dozen remains uncovered on Thursday were those of the last three children unaccounted for in the April 19 terrorist bombing. With the search at an end after 17 days, families will be allowed to gather at the site for one last, private remembrance, possibly this weekend."

After this, all that was left for those grieving was to try to move on, whether it was through faith in some future reunion or a hope for justice in the present. On June 14, the federal government tightened its case on McVeigh and Nichols, but it eliminated the search for "John Doe No. 2," concluding that the person in question likely had nothing to do with the bombings.

The cases against McVeigh and Nichols got their next big boost when Michael and Lori Fortier agreed to testify against the men in exchange for leniency for Michael and immunity for Lori. Michael admitted, "Prior to April 1995, McVeigh told me about the plans that he and Terry

Nichols had to blow up the Federal Building in Oklahoma City, Oklahoma. I did not as soon as possible make known my knowledge of the McVeigh and Nichols plot to any judge or other persons in civil authority. When F.B.I. agents questioned me later, about two days after the bombing, and during the next three days, I lied about my knowledge and concealed information. For example, I falsely stated that I had no knowledge of plans to bomb the federal building. I also gave certain items that I had received from McVeigh, including a bag of ammonium nitrate fertilizer, to a neighbor of mine so the items would not be found by law enforcement officers in a search of my residence."

On August 11, 1995, the grand jury hearing the case against McVeigh and Nichols returned an indictment: "Beginning on or about September 13, 1994 and continuing thereafter until on or about April 19, 1995...TIMOTHY JAMES McVEIGH and TERRY LYNN NICHOLS...did knowingly, intentionally, willfully and maliciously conspire, combine and agree together and with others unknown to the Grand Jury to use a weapon of mass destruction, namely an explosive bomb placed in a truck (a "truck bomb"), against persons within the United States and against property that was owned and used by the United States...resulting in death, grievous bodily injury and destruction of the building...It was the object of the conspiracy to kill and injure innocent persons and to damage property of the United States...As intended by McVEIGH and NICHOLS, the truck bomb explosion resulted in death and personal injury and the destruction of the Alfred P. Murrah Federal Building, located within the Western District of Oklahoma."

On October 20, Attorney General Janet Reno announced that she had ordered the government's prosecutors to seek the death penalty if McVeigh and Nichols were convicted. McVeigh's lawyer, Stephen Jones, noted, "The news hardly comes as a surprise. The attorney general and the president announced they would seek the death penalty before they even knew who the defendants were. ... We will mount our attack on the obvious pre-judgment of the case." Of course, given the national mood and the fact that the case against McVeigh was solid, technicalities were all that Jones had to work with. On December 1, he persuaded the 10th Circuit Court of Appeals to remove Judge Wayne Alley of Oklahoma and put the case under the jurisdiction of Judge Richard Matsch in Denver. Nearly three months later, Matsch ordered the trial itself moved to Denver, since he felt that the people of Oklahoma were too prejudiced to offer McVeigh a fair trial. In October 1996, Matsch ordered that McVeigh and Nichols be tried separately, and that McVeigh be tried first. This move may very well have saved Nichols' life.

On February 28, 1997, the public and the courts were shocked when the *Dallas Morning News* published an article with allegedly obtained documents that quoted McVeigh as confessing to the bombing. Particularly shocking was a quote from someone present at a July 1995 interview. When asked why he didn't just bomb the building at night, the staffer reported, "McVeigh looked directly into my eyes and told me, 'That would not have gotten the point across to the government. We needed a body count to make our point.'" The article also reported, "McVeigh again insisted that he was the one who drove the Ryder truck. ... McVeigh stated that James Nichols had no knowledge about the bombing as far as he knew, but that he didn't know what Terry Nichols might have told brother James."

For a time, it appeared as though these leaked remarks could derail the government's plans for the case, but the process went forward and jury selection began on March 31, 1997. The prosecution then made its opening statements, during which Joseph Hartzler referenced an envelope Officer Hanger had found in McVeigh's car the day he stopped him. "Enclosed in that envelope were slips of paper bearing statements that McVeigh had clipped from books and newspapers. And one of them was a quotation that -- from a book that McVeigh had copied. ...and he highlighted this -- 'The real value of our attacks today lies in the psychological impact, not in the immediate casualties.' Another slip of paper...reads, in part, 'When the government fears the people, there is liberty.' ... And hand-printed beneath those printed words, in McVeigh's handwriting, are the words...'Maybe now there will be liberty.' These documents are virtually a manifesto declaring McVeigh's intention. Everyone in this great nation has a right to think and believe, speak whatever they want. We are not prosecuting McVeigh because we don't like his thoughts or his beliefs or even his speech; we're prosecuting him because his hatred boiled into violence, and his violence took the lives of innocent men and women and children. And the reason we'll introduce evidence of his thoughts, as disclosed by those writings and others, is because they reveal his premeditation and his intent, and intent is an element of the crime that we must prove."

In response, the defense asserted, "I believe that when you see the evidence in this case, you will conclude that the investigation of the Alfred P. Murrah Building lasted about two weeks. The investigation to build the case against Timothy McVeigh lasted about two years. But within 72 hours after suspicion first centered on Mr. McVeigh. We will prove to you that even then, the Government knew, the FBI agents in the case, that the pieces of the puzzle were not coming together; that there was something terribly wrong, something missing. And as Paul Harvey says, our evidence will be the rest of the story."

Over the next month, the prosecution presented 137 witnesses, all of whom offered evidence against McVeigh. Then the defense took over, spending less than a week calling 25 witnesses. The two sides made their closing arguments on May 29 and the case was turned over to the jury. After just a few days of deliberation, they found McVeigh guilty on June 2 on all 11 counts against him. In thanking them for their service, the judge observed, "Members of the jury, you have determined by your verdict that the evidence established the guilt of Timothy McVeigh on these charges beyond a reasonable doubt of crimes for which death is a possible punishment. Whether Mr. McVeigh should be put to death for these crimes is a question to be answered by the jury serving as the conscience of the community. Although Congress has given this responsibility exclusively to the jury, the applicable statute and the Constitution command that you must exercise your discretion by following a specific procedure and give careful and thoughtful consideration to information characterized as 'aggravating and mitigating factors' to be presented now in a court hearing that is in a sense an extension or continuation of the trial...."

After more than a week of arguments for and against executing McVeigh, the jury decided unanimously on June 13, 1997 to sentence him to death. The judge announced, "Timothy James McVeigh, pursuant to the jury verdict returned on June 2, 1997, finding you guilty on all 11 counts of the indictment, the defendant is adjudged guilty of each of the following offenses: A conspiracy to use a weapon of mass destruction as charged in Count One, the use of a weapon of mass destruction as charged in Count Two, destruction by explosive as charged in Count Three, and first degree murder as charged in Counts Four through Eleven. Pursuant to the Federal Death Penalty Act of 1994, appearing in 18 United States Code Sections 3591 to 3596 and the special findings of the jury returned on June 13, 1997, and the jury's unanimous vote recommending that the defendant shall be sentenced to death, it is the judgment of the Court that the defendant, Timothy James McVeigh, is sentenced to death on each of the 11 counts of the indictment."

A picture of the supermax prison in Colorado where McVeigh was incarcerated alongside the Unabomber and Ramzi Yousef on "Bomber's Row"

While McVeigh's attorneys continued to appeal his conviction and the sentence, Terry Nichols was tried during the fall of 1997 and convicted on of most of the counts against him on December 23. However, he was found "not guilty" of actually using a weapon of mass destruction, and when the jury deliberated on his sentence, they could not agree on the death penalty. The *Washington Post* reported, "There was no evidence that Nichols had rented the Ryder truck used to carry the bomb to Oklahoma City, and there was no one who could positively identify him as the purchaser of the two tons of ammonium nitrate, the major component in the bomb. Most problematic for the government was the compelling fact that

Nichols was at home in Kansas when McVeigh detonated the truck." Therefore, Nichols was sentenced on June 4, 1998 to life without parole. By this time, Michael Fortier had already began serving a 12 year sentence for his role in the conspiracy.

Each of McVeigh's appeals failed, and the Supreme Court ultimately refused to hear his case. On July 13, 1999 he was moved to the federal penitentiary in Terre Haute, Indiana to await execution. CBS reporter Ed Bradley interviewed him there on March 12, 2000 and later said, "Well, his rationalization, is because of the policies of this government. And it keys on what happened at Waco, and I guess Ruby Ridge, and I mean that is what he thinks is wrong with this government. And that this government is working against people he would regard as patriots. I'm not [surprised he wants to die]. I think that -- I think that he feels that this is the best way for him to go. I read something of what he planned to say -- at least, what he has said he plans to say before he dies in his last words, that he is the captain of his ship. He is the captain of his fate. And in that sense, in that he has said, I'm going to waive all my appeals, kill me -- in that sense he feels that he is deciding his fate."

A picture of the penitentiary in Terre Haute

While at the penitentiary in Terre Haute, McVeigh wrote a letter that discussed the bombing, as well as an attempt to justify his actions:

"The administration has said that Iraq has no right to stockpile chemical or biological weapons ("weapons of mass destruction") — mainly because they have used them in the past.

"Well, if that's the standard by which these matters are decided, then the U.S. is the nation that set the precedent. The U.S. has stockpiled these same weapons (and more) for over 40 years. The U.S. claims this was done for deterrent purposes during its 'Cold War' with the Soviet Union. Why, then, it is invalid for Iraq to claim the same reason (deterrence) with respect to Iraq's (real) war with, and the continued threat of, its neighbor Iran?

"The administration claims that Iraq has used these weapons in the past. We've all seen the pictures that show a Kurdish woman and child frozen in death from the use of chemical weapons. But, have you ever seen those pictures juxtaposed next to pictures from Hiroshima or Nagasaki?

"I suggest that one study the histories of World War I, World War II and other 'regional conflicts' that the U.S. has been involved in to familiarize themselves with the use of "weapons of mass destruction."

Remember Dresden? How about Hanoi? Tripoli? Baghdad? What about the big ones — Hiroshima and Nagasaki? (At these two locations, the U.S. killed at least 150,000 non-combatants — mostly women and children — in the blink of an eye. Thousands more took hours, days, weeks or months to die).

"If Saddam is such a demon, and people are calling for war crimes charges and trials against him and his nation, why do we not hear the same cry for blood directed at those responsible for even greater amounts of 'mass destruction' — like those responsible and involved in dropping bombs on the cities mentioned above?

"The truth is, the U.S. has set the standard when it comes to the stockpiling and use of weapons of mass destruction…

"Hypocrisy when it comes to the death of children? In Oklahoma City, it was family convenience that explained the presence of a day-care center placed between street level and the law enforcement agencies which occupied the upper floors of the building. Yet, when discussion shifts to Iraq, any day-care center in a government building instantly becomes 'a shield.' Think about it.

"When considering morality and 'mens rea', in light of these facts, I ask: Who are the true barbarians? ...

"I find it ironic, to say the least, that one of the aircraft used to drop such a bomb on Iraq is dubbed 'The Spirit of Oklahoma.' This leads me to a final, and unspoken, moral hypocrisy regarding the use of weapons of mass destruction.

"When a U.S. plane or cruise missile is used to bring destruction to a foreign people, this nation rewards the bombers with applause and praise. What a convenient way to absolve these killers of any responsibility for the destruction they leave in their wake.

"Unfortunately, the morality of killing is not so superficial. The truth is, the use of a truck, a plane or a missile for the delivery of a weapon of mass destruction does not alter the nature of the act itself.

"These are weapons of mass destruction — and the method of delivery matters little to those on the receiving end of such weapons.

"Whether you wish to admit it or not, when you approve, morally, of the bombing of foreign targets by the U.S. military, you are approving of acts morally equivalent to the bombing in Oklahoma City..."

On January 16, 2001, McVeigh announced that he was dropping the rest of his appeals, and the court set his execution date for four months later. Then, suddenly, there was a twist in the case when new documents came to light that the Justice Department admitted had not been shared previously with the defense. The new Attorney General, John Ashcroft, insisted that the execution be postponed for one month so that the defense could have a chance to review the more than 4,000 pages of documents.

On June 1, McVeigh announced that he had changed his mind and would in fact continue the appeals process, but a week later, having heard from all sides, the appeals court again denied McVeigh's stay. Before his sentence was carried out, he ruminated on the idea of an afterlife and claimed, "If there is a hell, then I'll be in good company with a lot of fighter pilots who also had to bomb innocents to win the war."

Timothy McVeigh was executed by lethal injection on June 11, 2001. For his last words, he chose the poem "Invictus" by the Victorian poet William Earnest Henley.

"Out of the night that covers me,
Black as the pit from pole to pole,
I thank whatever gods may be
For my unconquerable soul.

"In the fell clutch of circumstance
I have not winced nor cried aloud.
Under the bludgeonings of chance
My head is bloody, but unbowed.

"Beyond this place of wrath and tears
Looms but the Horror of the shade,
And yet the menace of the years

Finds, and shall find me, unafraid.

"It matters not how strait the gate,
How charged with punishments the scroll,
I am the master of my fate:
I am the captain of my soul."

Family members of the victims were on hand to witness McVeigh's execution, but it didn't necessarily bring closure, with more than one bemoaning the fact that McVeigh didn't seem the least bit remorseful. In reference to the fact McVeigh declined to give a final statement just before his execution, Jay Sawyer complained, "Without saying a word, he got the final word." Larry Whicher, who lost his brother, said McVeigh had "a totally expressionless, blank stare. He had a look of defiance and that if he could, he'd do it all over again." Disturbingly, McVeigh went so far as to ask that his remains be located at the site of the memorial for the bombing, an act even he ultimately deemed "too vengeful, too raw, too cold."

McVeigh was gone, but victims were still upset that Nichols wasn't. Disappointed that the jury did not give Nichols the death penalty, the State of Oklahoma successfully appealed to try him on 161 counts of first degree murder. The trial took place in the spring of 2004 and led to more than 150 witnesses being called. In the end, Nichols was found guilty, but the jury in Oklahoma could not agree on a death sentence. CNN reported, "Nichols sat straight in his chair Friday as the jury foreman handed a note to Taylor that said, 'We will not be able to reach a unanimous verdict.' 'Sometimes this is how trials end up,' [Judge Steven] Taylor said. Nichols' mother, sister and ex-wife sat in the front row on one side of the courtroom, while bombing victims and their families sat on the other side of the aisle. 'This is unbelievable to me,' said the relative of one of the bombing victims, pointing to all the evidence presented by prosecutors. The jury returned to the courtroom twice Friday so its foreman could tell the judge the panel appeared hopelessly divided. The second time, Taylor told the jurors they could resume their talks or give up. After deliberating another hour, jurors returned to the courtroom with their final decision. ... 'Each and every one of these people died so [Nichols and McVeigh] could make a political statement,' prosecutor Sandra Elliott told the jury Wednesday in her closing arguments. Defense lawyers described Nichols as the pawn of a 'dominant, manipulative and controlling' McVeigh. The prosecution and defense called 87 witnesses over five days of testimony in the penalty phase of the trial, many of them relatives still grieving over their losses nine years ago. Nichols' attorney, Creekmore Wallace, urged jurors not to be swayed by 'that flood of tears, that flood of pain' related by victims who testified."

With nothing else he could do, Judge Taylor used his own authority to add 160 more life sentences to the one Nichols already had.

Online Resources

Other 20th century history titles by Charles River Editors

Other titles about the Oklahoma City Bombing on Amazon

Bibliography

City of Oklahoma City Document Management (1996). Final Report: Alfred P. Murrah Federal Building Bombing April 19, 1995. Stillwater, OK: Department of Central Services Central Printing Division.

Giordano, Geraldine (2003). The Oklahoma City Bombing. New York: The Rosen Publishing Group, Inc.

Hoffman, David (1998). The Oklahoma City Bombing and the Politics of Terror. Feral House.

Key, Charles, State Representative (2001). The Final Report of the Bombing of the Alfred P. Murrah Building. Oklahoma City, Oklahoma: The Oklahoma Bombing Investigation Committee.

Michel, Lou; Dan Herbeck (2001). American Terrorist: Timothy McVeigh & The Oklahoma City Bombing. New York: Regan Books.

Oklahoma Today (2005). 9:02 am, April 19, 1995: The Official Record of the Oklahoma City Bombing. Oklahoma City: Oklahoma Today.

Serano, Richard A. (1998). One of Ours: Timothy McVeigh and the Oklahoma City Bombing. New York: W. W. Norton & Company.

Sherrow, Victoria (1998). The Oklahoma City Bombing: Terror in the Heartland. Springfield, N.J.: Enslow Publishers.

Made in the USA
Las Vegas, NV
28 January 2023

66410382R00030